REWIRED: Friendly Street Poets 32

Maggie Emmett arrived in Australia in 1967, on the last boat through the Suez Canal during that Middle East War. She was educated at Grammar School in Berkshire, England. In her past working lives she was an Intensive Care Sister, a Casualty RN, and an academic at the Uni of Adelaide. Now, she runs an editing & communications business. She pays her social rent working on the Friendly St Board as their Publishing Officer, Liaison Officer with the Art Gallery of SA and the Radio Adelaide Coordinator. She has two daughters, three grandchildren and a poodle.

Gaetano Aiello is the current Convenor and Treasurer of Friendly St Poets Inc., roles he has assumed for three years. He comes from a migrant Italian family and is a first generation Australian. Educated at Campbelltown High School and the University of Adelaide. He is a legal practitioner specialising in the areas of Trust, Wills and Disputed Estates. He runs every day and competes in Athletics. He is President of the Western Districts Athletic Club and Chairperson of the Clubs Council of Athletics South Australia. He has been writing poetry since the age of sixteen and reads regularly at Friendly St meetings. He is happily married and has one son.

REWIRED
Friendly Street Poets 32

Edited by
Maggie Emmett and Gaetano Aiello

Friendly Street Poets in association with Wakefield Press

Friendly Street Poets Incorporated
PO Box 43 Rundle Mall
Adelaide
South Australia 5000
www.friendlystreetpoets.org.au

in association with

Wakefield Press
1 The Parade West
Kent Town
South Australia 5067
www.wakefieldpress.com.au

First published 2008

Cover photograph copyright © Ben Searcy, www.bensearcy.com.au
Cover design by Clinton Ellicott, Wakefield Press
Edited by M.L. Emmett & Gaetano Aiello, Friendly Street Poets Inc.
Typeset by Clinton Ellicott, Wakefield Press
Printed and bound by Hyde Park Press, Adelaide

ISBN 978 1 86254 790 2

**Government
of South Australia**

Arts SA

Friendly Street Poets Inc. is supported
by the **South Australian Government**
through **Arts SA**.

Contents

Thank you
to all the poets who read and submitted material for the book
and equally the enthusiastic, supportive audience
for actively listening.
It is this reciprocal relationship
that is the dynamic force
that feeds Friendly St

Thank you
for the continuing support of Arts SA
who keep our publishing program financially alive

Acknowledgement

Friendly St Poets acknowledges the Kaurna people
as the orginal owners and custodians of the Adelaide Plains.

Preface

Reading to a live audience is an electrifying experience. It's challenging and exciting. It takes courage and personal integrity to risk offering your words to an audience. Yet on the first Tuesday of the month, new poets arrive ready to snatch their four minutes at the open microphone and read at the longest running uncensored poetry reading group in the southern hemisphere. In 2007, 624 poets seized this opportunity and read over 1250 poems at Friendly St meetings, including our two extra readings at Port Noarlunga and Salisbury.

Friendly St meetings are gathering places for poets from all over South Australia each one prepared to share their poetry. Regardless of age, gender, ethnicity, cultural background and ideology, our common goal is the writing, reading and publication of poetry. There may be a saxaphone, a flute, a guitar, percussive terra cotta pots or a CD of Handel's Water Music gently playing in the background, but the foreground pulses and sparks with poetic energy.

Form and content, style and substance are as diverse as the voices we hear. Some are quiet and tentative as they read for the first time; others are confident, strong and certain. There are voices that shout out pain and anger, demanding attention. There are gentle, sibilant voices and almost whispering voices that sing their dreams and secrets. There are tortured, wailing voices that tell of loss and war, confronting us with their courage. Punctuated, perfect pausing voices that mark and measure every word. Mischevious, naughty voices that surprise us, making us grin, giggle and hoot with laughter. And always there are the words, the crafted well chosen words that make the poem do its work.

As we started the long editing process, we were mindful of the quality and history of the Friendly St brand name we represented, of the wisdom and skill of editors before us. 777 poems were submitted for publication and in such a bumper year, poems had to earn their selection. As editors, we experienced the sheer pleasure of the close reading task, but then came the pain of choosing. It is never possible to include the work of every reader. This anthology is not a perfect record of the year of poems, but an impression of its strengths.

The book we constructed contains poems written by a broad range of poets, from the 21 newly emerging, previously unpublished poets, to long established poets. It is a volume clearly demonstrating the vibrant, thriving state of Friendly St and the depth of its poetic talent.

Passion is the current that runs through this book. Words, voices and memories are the power lines that connect us and hold us together in networks and grids. Rewired and ready for the next energy zap!

Maggie Emmett and Gaetano Aiello

WET EVENING IN RUNDLE STREET

Again
the sky has
dropped
behind the loose skin
of dark clouds

Rain
is
falling
on some streets
and not others

Cranes perch
awkwardly
over
their unfinished buildings
while the night hangs
half
off
its hinge

Along
footpaths
umbrellas have mushroomed
out of bodies

Windscreen wipers
flap
with the fierceness
of migrating birds
taking flight

Thrown
against
the café
and bookshop windows

the voices of rain
are broken
and its long sentences
are lost down
gutters

Now
only
a couple
of Italian boys
on scooters
are left
alfresco

Above
the city
a few stars
are being rewired

Between buildings
the night
has hung
out
its moon
to drip dry

JULES LEIGH KOCH
Published in ARTSTATE

JIGSAW

It must have been the way the shapes and spaces
responded to my fingers and gave hints
of a final locking into one that pleased me.
Alone, pillowed in my bed in the sickroom,
I put the thousand pieces on an old tin tray
and began to create a city within a frame.

Golden-glazed Venice, where a shaft of sunlight
gives weight to spire and dome and *palazzo*
and sunset clouds are mirrored in the bay.
Listen to the blare of trumpets, the round echo
of a bell and always the incessant lapping
of water at the base of a flight of stairs.
As a breeze stirs, pennants in regal purple
ribbon the wind, while in the foreground
three gondolas with three bent figures
to guide them, slip forward and break clear.

A strange stillness here – a celebration
of the sound of silence in the colours of a dream
Even today, these pieces of perfumed wood
with there neat irregularities tangle in my mind.
There's a conspiracy to outwit my right hand,
until confusion gives way to promise
and they spread out again before me,
to connect and precisely join together as one.

ELAINE BARKER

BELFAST

Above the empty shipyards, the two cranes,
Sampson and Goliath,
like two great brooding birds, are etched on the skyline.
Three generations ago, Titanic left here,
carrying the pride and aspirations of a generation.
Now, those forced to leave, like my father,
return in the shape of their children,
who know nothing of being Irish.

The tour bus doesn't only take us
to where Titanic was built,
but to burnt out police stations,
murals and barbed wire.
We see the streets of boarded-up houses
where my father lived –

I read the inscription on my grandparents' grave,
in the tidy graveyard at Grey Abbey;
sit in a polished pew
in the church where my father once sat;
touch the stones of the house where he lived –
it is no use,
I am a stranger still.

BARBARA PRESTON

ECHOES OF EMPIRE
(overheard in a Dublin cafe)

Plum ripe with imperial tones,
the voice demanded attention
powered by the smooth motor
of assumed privilege:

I bristled instinctively,
reacting to a history
slewed by the bias
of a bruised nation:

her folk memory and mine
opposite poles of a common Irishness

BRIAN FOX

LADY OF THE MOUNTAINS

Fjallkonan, the symbol of Iceland

I think of you often,
Lady of the Mountains,
with your rising gold crown
reflecting in the white of your veil
like the midnight sun on snow-covered peaks.

I think of you and your gown of black silk
that shines like frozen rhyolite
and lava,
fashioned into fearsome images
of trolls and ancient gods.

I think of your belt of gold,
red gold,
that falls heavy from your waist
like liquid fire,
like red hot magma
pouring.

I think of the flowers that flow in golden borders
around the hem of your garment,
reminding me
of your bright summer nights
when birds and sun forget to sleep
and salmon fly your falls upstream.

I think of you, motherland
often.

YR HAM

A BITTER TASTE

Eat Creole Jambalaya in Antoine's,
buy pralines from Tante Clementine,
elle est une chef magnifique!
Listen to jazz at The House of Blues
on a burning, heavy night on Bourbon Street.

In the bayous alligators snap,
Confederates fly the flag and dream.
They planned to free Napoleon, bring him
to New Orleans and Vive La Revolution!
But History is full of snakes that bite.

In inner courtyards, fountains trickle,
hear the clop of horses' hooves.
Fans, precisely manic, beat and beat.
They promised Southern hospitality and power
then left Napoleon exiled in Elba.

I met a man in the Cajun bayou,
who had Napoleon's black and piercing eyes.
A friend of Fidel Castro, he had lived in
Cuba with hurricanes, cigars and lusty women.
He taught me to eat po-boys, crawfish and beignets,
asked me to stay to share his chariot of skeletons.

I rode pillion on the Harley, stared at the
bristling hairs on my Napoleon's neck.
Like Marie Laveau, the voodoo queen, we
curved and plunged into the shadows, the clock
shriked five and we listened to ghosts groan.
Time has kissed resolutions with moist, lying lips.

TESS DRIVER
Published in ArtState

CROIX DE LA ROCHETTE

In France, the kitchen window-sill
doubled as an extension of the fridge.
Strawberries, butter and cream stood side by side
basking in the cool moist air.

For breakfast we ate walnut bread
and drank coffee in large bowls
bringing its warmth to our lips
with both hands, like a lover.

At midday on the dot we dined
on food and wine refined through years
of happy gatherings in gardens
and the market place.

When the angelus rang out at seven
we gathered in the strawberries
sipped on memories of a summer's day
and knew we were in heaven.

JILL GLOYNE

EID 2005

A wrong turn swept us
from the freeway
past factories into residential
and industrial landscape.

Bickering, we searched for the way
until above houses and factories,
over multi-coloured silks and brocades
like palaces from the Arabian Nights
minarets soared.

Again I heard chanting
standing with my sisters
arrayed in rainbow colours,
and I smelt the sweet smell
of incense wafting at the top
of the staircase
like the entrance to paradise.

JUDITH AHMED

BAIA DOS TIGRES, ANGOLA

I can envisage a bay
with shifting tides and currents
and tiger stripes of sandbars.
The name suggests to sailors
that they sail into the bay
as one would walk into a jungle
in which it was known
there were tigers.
The name also shows
that the Portuguese Navigators
knew what tigers were
long before they reached India.

GARTH DUTTON

MEMORIES
Inarlanga Pass in the West MacDonnell Ranges National Park
Northern Territory

The ancient seas have come
     and gone a time or two
   with bone-dry rock their lasting testament.
On broken sandstone slabs
     sand ripples yet remain
   the last wave-remnants from a bygone shore.
And from those long-gone seas
     shell fossils give a glimpse
   of ancient life that lived its ancient way.
We walk our winding path
     along a turning gorge
   where cycad palms still cling to shaded spots:
a fading vestige they
     of wetter centuries
   still living fossils from a time long past.
Along this pathway too
     Inarlanga elders
   in their day did pass to sacred business.
Like silent watching ghosts
     that stand beside our way
   these memories remain within the land.
Then from the gorge we walk
     into a wider space
   red country greener-touched by recent rains:
a rolling range of grass
     amongst the scattered trees
   a pleasing prospect to the human eye.

Pre-human ancestors
      before the Pleistocene
   first walked upright in such savannah scenes.
Those landscapes nurtured us
     and gave us human form.
In mind and body both
     they shaped our human lives.
For reasons scarcely sensed
    we revel in such scenes –
  a life forgotten now
    remembered in our genes.

LAWRENCE E. JOHNSON

LUBRA CREEK, KANGAROO ISLAND

for the Indigenous women who were stolen by sealers and
whalers to live and work on Kangaroo Island

there is nothing that says you were here,
the mallee continues to grow in a tangle
with its gold-tipped crowns of green
and messy bark hanging down like scrolls,
that I wish I knew how to read

there is nothing that says you were here,
it is cool and muted as it was
the creek curving to a breathing sea
out   and   in
the mainland beckoning like a mirage

there is nothing that says you were here,
even though you were tied and lashed
for trying to escape across Backstairs Passage,
flesh sliced from your buttocks like a seal's –
the blood is all gone now

there is nothing that says you were here,
but the minka bird – messenger of death,
who wails overhead as its ancestors did before.

MOLLY MURN

BURIAL BONES

Tasmania, May 2007

drone of didgeridoo
mourn to dark cloud
on spears of time
ghost of grief
cleansed by grey smoke
of gum leaf

wallaby mob stand
like spirit warriors
as roots of eucalyptus and history
keep beat on the skin of tribal land
barren dreaming womb weeps
for her stolen children

sap of ancient gum bleed
in remembrance
tongue of Derwent River lash the shore
like a cat-o'-nine-tails
scarred the memory
of sorry business

COLLEEN SWEENEY

UNFOLDING

I find myself
unfolding in the Flinders
stretching from horizon
to blue-rimmed horizon
dissolving in the heat
cell-shocked with colour
cobalt, cerulean
and seven shades of ochre
explode complacency
here, there is no room
for dark thoughts
or pale
at night I lie
pinned to the ground
by points of starlight

returning to the city
I draw in
breath shallow
voice thin
eyes down
elbows in
contract
compress
dreams
into boxes
that break open
cannot contain
days that bellow bright
or nights of starsong

VERONICA SHANKS
Published in Arstate

NIMBIN

Nimbin nestled discreetly in the green folds
of the New England rain forest
a single street formed by a rough ribbon of tar
bordered by timber buildings grey with age
unpainted except where
artists have plied their craft,
one, the headquarters of the
Australian Marijuana Party
another, a butcher's shop
a surprise as expectations were for
a town of dope smoking vegans.

My friend parks his brand new Mercedes
between two rusty combi-vans
each a psychedelic memory of the sixties
I feel unsafe, intrusive, out of place
but people greet us good naturedly
the sweet perfume of dope pervades my senses
my friend informs me that
the local growers have been wiped out
supplies now come from South Australia
his manner suggests collective guilt.

It must be pension day
there is a long queue at the ATM
but it's the dogs that catch my eye
a mixed bunch of tick ridden hounds
sharing common ancestry with local dingoes
unregistered, uncollared, unappealing
and most likely unloved
trailing in slavering packs
behind a single bitch on heat
pink points of passion
proclaiming their pernicious intent.

There is a muted police presence
recently busy, I'm told
keeping their big city colleagues
and their drug dogs out of town
they have to keep the peace
but they do it their way
my wife asks a question
loudly, as she does when she is surprised
"Why are they burning so much incense?" she asks
locals turn their heads and smile
I feel a wave of affection for her innocence
I answer "Breathe deeply, darling, and enjoy."

KEN VINCENT

ROAD KILL

On the fox-free island
roadsides are lined
with furry carcasses
in varying states of decay.
Some bloated
their four legs
coffee-table splayed.
They are a pageant crowd
waving stiffly
at us, a cavalcade
of murderers.
My three year old niece
laughs and waves back.
'Look mummy,
it's smiling', she says,
pointing at the bared teeth
as a little cloud
of blowflies rises up
like glittering black
ticker-tape.

JUDE AQUILINA

QUARRY LAND, LEASED 'til 2020

In 1860
these green and teeming hills
lay dense with wood and herb,
with fur and scale and feather,
as warm with a million insects,
timber stood proud and dammed the banks
of liquid crystal streams

In 1960
these brown and leaching hills
lay clothed with bones and weeds –
thistles from Britain, olives from Greece,
Cape daisies crawl from quarry slag-heaps,
birds cancelled flight and soupy creeks stank
under scums of blue-green algae.

Towards 2020 . . .
these heat-hoven ancient hills
lie silent, resolute,
boxthorn skeletons creak in the breeze

but the natural course will not be undone –
here spins a leaf-green spider;
blooms a clump of candle flower;
winks a brown snake, at the new century's sun.

J.L. BAKER
New Poets 13

metaphor

mercurial skies
bleed tiger eyes
on a city parched.
rough winds flutter
from skeleton trees,
mute suicides
(lines without context)
scuffing a landscape
that's fifteen different
shades of grey,
big steps and
urban decay.

chills grip
while lines rip
in carrollian nonsense.
rivers of adrenalin
make shelter come
in strange costumes.
puddles tremble
but do not fill
without fifteen different
shades of grey,
big steps and
urban decay.

unexploded
and overloaded
in a city of punchlines.
caught in a metaphor
of limited success
and minor celebrity.
melbourne, i wear you
like a woollen jumper
that's fifteen different
shades of grey,
big steps and
urban decay.

KERRYN TREDREA

POETRY READING

In the front row trenches
words charge through the air
like tiny spit globule bullets
fired from fast forming mouths,
sparking my frontage.

I'm the front line soldier
never seeing behind my eyes
to the lines and lines
of verse staring
at the back of my head.

I ride fast,
with the mike as my bayonet,
aimed, to sound my words out
like whispers
to sweat your brow.

INDIGO

THE LIVES OF POEMS

Poems go to work on public transport
and come home
with gritty realism
pressed in the tread of their shoes.

Poems sit in airconditioned offices
in tottering towers
window watching,
waiting for the next plane to hit.

Poems go out for a day in the country
and come back
with the grandeur of nature
stuck in their hair.

Poems travel to foreign countries
and return with cases full
of human similarity vignettes
and postcard 'delicate miniatures'.
of scenic beauty.

Poems go on summer holidays
and come home sandy
with tidal urges
and the sound of sea in shells.

M.L. EMMETT

POETIC PEDICURE

Poetry should be read
    preferably aloud
    preferably to an audience
    preferably,
    but not necessarily

Poetry should not be restricted
    to beats per line
    beats called feet
    and counted

Poetry can though, be constructed by
    meter and rhyme
    measured and regular
    – or not

Iambic pentameter
Trochaic hexameter
Anapaestic dimeter.

Poetic pedicure
    just pass me the nail polish.

SARAH WAUCHOPE

I HATE POEMS

I hate poems
written specifically
for an occasion

I hate poems
so obscure
nobody understands them

I hate poems
that need explanation
or reference to Greek myth

I hate poems that rhapsodise
about sunsets or breasts
or figs

I hate poems
cobbled together
for anthologies

I hate poems
that are long
and repetitive

I hate poems like this.

JUDY DALLY

I hate poems
with a message so subtle
nobody gets it

I hate poems
that rhyme obviously
or don't rhyme, obviously

I hate poems
preceded by quotes
that are better than the poem

I hate poems
typed in a fog of alcohol
and self-recrimination

I hate poems
that are smart-arse and cocky
and written only for a laugh

I hate poems
that search desperately
for an ending

BETWEEN THE WORDS

I thought to unlock mysteries:
words on a page archaeological tools
excavating, brushing, sifting.

I thought the names of things
would pin them down – like carbon dating
fixing on a point in time;

that I could sidle up silently upon truth,
ambush it within parentheses
by a simple act of revelation.

I followed that path to its end,
turned back, returned many times
unearthing only fragments of the whole.

Language bleeds. Definitions mock borders.
Meaning bypasses manned checkpoints,
slips unseen between the lines.

So many hoarse shouts echo between the words,
so many silences, so many unspoken truths.

DAVID ADÈS

THE BOOKS WITH BROKEN SPINES

(at the Story of Berlin Museum)

As I stepped into the hallway I was counting on
a flight of marble stairs, neat rows of artefacts,
objects of beauty set behind glass
or pictures at eye-level, well-lit.
When I looked down I saw
my shoes passing over a very smooth floor
where books were sealed in clear resin,
like bodies lined up in a burial pit.
And in the dusty half-light books and pamphlets
were strewn about like rubbish
in the void or were piled against the wall:
Otto Dix, George Grosz, Brecht and Chagall,
Engels and Lenin, Thomas Mann and Sigmund Freud,
'All Quiet on the Western Front' nudging 'Das Kapital'.
Despite the raw stillness there
my thoughts were fixed on banners and flames
and the blackness of jack boots.
I was not expecting the tangle of volumes
to shout or cry out;
books have always suffered silently.
But had I stopped longer I might have heard
the lament of the books with broken spines.
Or the snap of breaking bones.
That first day, I heard muffled words only
and the slow march or shuffle of feet.

ELAINE BARKER

STONES OF THE GIBBER DESERT

Like a necklace of gibber stones
I wear my life. Perfectly
pitted and indented with age
and memories, weighing me down,
yet constant and true; these are my companions.

Coloured as dried blood
familiar with extremes,
cold and heat, no moderation.
Desert winds have shaped and polished
a minute landscape of loss and pain.

Determined, I chose each one
in full pleasure and pride.
Now my life's decoration, they rise
and fall with my heart, take on my skin
till there is no difference between us.

ANNE CHAPPEL

UNTOUCHABLE

Looking outward to the stars
I sometimes try to understand
the tangle of myself within all this.

Between untouchable distance
and the folding of the air
our bodies are just serendipity

The night-time of sky
still fills my mind and redefines
the earth that holds me.

And in this cool, blue evening
I too can seem transparent
with sensing my way beyond
the deepest stretch of thought.
The disappearing sun,
the floating moon
are in my breath.

They say, when it's all added up
we stand on almost nothing,
held by the imagination
of the smallest things,
which court each other
constantly – that's all.
Our foothold an illusion
a magus trick, just
the folly of a trillion tiny things.

JO DEY

HOLDING THE NIGHT

In the morning, sleep abandons me
onto the shore of consciousness.
I lie curled up, benign
and hold the night around me.
The Black Theatre of dream
erases its shapes and colours
until they are untouchable as
a whisper of scented smoke.

Thus each night finds its own
Quixotic consolation.

Soon the relentless continuity of days
is pacing back and forth
outside my window.

JO DEY

DREAM-POD

The bubble had burst, but the dream
was still there, the inside of a balloon
floating unprotected.

She sidled her way through market
alleys to the basket weaver who coiled
balloon strings and feathers into a cot.

She lay her dreams bare. Seeing this,
the glass blower melted the oranges,
yellows and reds of fireworks

into a dome cover that drew soft heat
from the sun's breath. The tailor
forgave silk off cuts for cushions,

and a young boy who found the pin
in a doorway, placed within
the dream-pod a pebble from his pocket.

She closed the lid and turning
to contemplate the ocean, bumped
a crouched woman wrapped white

in ashen dust, spinning tears
around teacups. "Time", she said,
"Time will make it a pearl."

INDIGO

CIRCLE

I know that
the moment of departure
is the first moment of arrival,

that as soon
as I leave you
I will begin my return to you.

I am not deluded
by the motion of planes trains buses
or by the curvature of the earth,

by unspecified distances
visitations to the past
the slow peeling of the future's mask.

I will not confuse
absent faces with those I meet
or meet again.

I am a circle
endlessly circling
running rings around myself,

returning always
to the same destination
with you at its centre.

DAVID ADÈS
Single Poet Series

FLYING

I began flying before I grew wings.
In those days I could just swim
in the air or zoom about as if
I had jets on my feet.
That was after I left school
and began growing into myself.

Flying is a very good way
to escape pursuers, men
you aren't interested in,
or embarassing situations –
anything dangerous or awkward
and I'd take to the air.

Then one day, a very nasty man
was chasing me, so I took off.
It was such a relief to be able
to get away like that.
Trouble was he started flying after me
and that was that; I never flew again –

even though, eventually, I grew these wings.

BELINDA BROUGHTON

70s DRIVE-IN

the huge screen embraces our car as
its silent movie caresses love-locked hips,
and like stars winking in this metal galaxy
it backlights our desire

smoke signals pout and kiss through open windows
the haze seduces
puffing us towards a teenage nirvana of lust
and candy-wrapped Hitchcock in the fog

intermission; we adjourn to swagger in neon's glow
world weary from all that sex and death,
buy burgers, and hang out
with fellow travellers of the flesh

then roll back, gorged and sleepless
to dip fingers into closing credits
change gears
and tune in to the home station . . .
drive back to childhood and curfew.

JENNY TOUNE

SHEETS

sometimes
transferring sheets
from washing machine to basket
is in itself a poem
or a prayer

sun and wind
dance their spirit into the fabric
so that smoothing it
onto the bed
becomes a benediction

last night, my love
lay curled in these sheets
moonlight kissed
his eyelids and his hair
so did I
drink his sweet breath
and tasted salt

old hands
folding sheets
touch briefly
remember noontime loving
burnished bright
with the blessings of time

VERONICA SHANKS

ORDINARY LOVERS

When we kissed
there were no fireworks
over Sydney Harbour
and the Yarra River
did not turn blue
and snowflakes
did not transform
into tear drops
and peach trees in China
did not blossom.

When we kissed
we were just two people
with naked hearts
and trembling fingers
clinging to a moment
we did not want to end.
The nightingales were speechless
the owls lost their wisdom.
Maybe there is no genius
in a kiss, just a hunger

a thousand centuries old
and a need for comfort
willow trees can not fathom.
When we kissed
the moon did not scream
and the stars stuttered
but your eyes were bright
looking into mine
searching for answers
to questions I did not understand.

We were both dumb with love
and we didn't mind at all.

MICHAEL CRANE

BEANIE ON THE MOON

Regardless of warnings from *The Police*
about walking on the moon
tonight, anything seems possible.
Aglow with umbra
and globally-warmed penumbra
there it hangs, like a giant plum:

a delicious treat, ripe to be picked,
to be plucked and cradled
carefully stowed away
beyond the outstretched arms
of *Eucalyptus* this or *Eucalyptus* that
dark along the razorback ridge.

Tonight, anything is possible:
perhaps we will magically rise
to float in geosynchronous orbit
above crystalline cirrus mists
above circumpolar auroras
across the breaking diapause.

Perhaps, we will end up like
astronauts, out of earthly reach
untethered from our mother ship,
bathed with continental afterglow
at intersections of curvilinear space
all but lost to mission control.

Yet, as we nestle warm together
unharmed by approaching lunar frosts
our cloaks of emu feathers
are light around our weightlessness;
our beanies, packed with bodyshine
are snug about our ears.

IAN GIBBINS

SAFE BET

When they replaced the gutters
the salesman said
the job would be good for fifteen years.
You think that should just about see us out.
I'm not so sure – by then you'll be eighty
but I'll just be a spritely seventy two.

Next, we ordered a rainwater tank
it sits on its stand, squat, green
in solemn hope it *will* rain again.
Delivery man tells us
the tank's guaranteed for twenty five years.
You look at me, we laugh, and I wonder.

Will you still want me to hold the ladder steady
make your knobbly knees knock if I
slither my hand up the leg of your shorts
when you climb those steps to clear the gutters,
over twenty five years, when you'll be ninety
but I'll just be a spritely eighty two?

VERONICA COOKSON

DOUBLE CONCERTO

I play *adagio*, you play *con brio*,
the critics applaud your brilliant display.
Is this what is called a double concerto?

You run the *arpeggios* where I cannot follow,
your fingers flying, up and away.
While you play *con brio*, I play *adagio*.

Soft pedal depressed, the movement is slow
my two hands crossing in a lonely sashay.
I know by heart this double concerto.

But a ballad of love has a different tempo
to this set piece we so often replay,
where I play *adagio*, you play *con brio*.

Out of time and each note *staccato*,
my *piano* drowned by your *forte*
we struggle to play this double concerto.

When we come to the end of the final rondo,
there is no encore and no bouquet.
I've played *adagio*, you've played *con brio* –
it's a difficult piece this double concerto.

MARY BRADLEY

LIKE FINE WINE

Sweet on the palette
Medium to full length . . .
length inevitably does matter
some claim otherwise
Clarity, flawless on the eyes
I can see right through him
he has nothing to hide
Complex characteristics emerge
thwarting my evaluation
harder to read than I thought
nevertheless it keeps me eager
willingly trailing his scent
past first and secondary aromas
allured with sensual plumes
like breadcrumbs
they draw me closer
truly defining magnetism
never loosing its girth
as you improve with age
slowly revealing yourself
as you breath easy
stripping away the sediments
of self-consciousness
leaving something decanted
at peace and sensitive

ANDREW ELLERY

light

a rattling
of children

through you
front of

the house
screen door

swings, the wire
punctured with

a generation
of finger

holes poked
& mended

& repoked
until a moment

of grace
a lifting

of shoulders
for the patterns

arranged on
the hallway

floor when
light

catches
as unskilled

emotions would
calm a just born child

RORY HARRIS

PROLOGUE

You are nowhere near ready to appear,
to emerge from around the lip of cervix

yet your light already shines
upon so many upturned faces

and all my shadows
have disappeared

CHILD

We threaded you
through the eye of possibility
into being

BIRTH
(Orli Shai Adès – 9 February 2007)

Stone dropped into a
still lake: splash! A lifetime of
ripples spreading out.

DAVID ADÈS

IN MY MIND'S EYE (FOR JASON)

Every room
is full of dark.

But I can feel
the beat
of thoughts
Sense
the moods
of minds
know
the shape of faces

I recognise
every voice
remember
every lyric

In my mind's eye
I know
every corner
of every room.

JUDY DALLY

THE CHILD WITH AUTISM PLAYS

The boy with psychotic
tendencies
is chasing the voices
in his head
along the fence-line

Masking his face
with one hand
he talks excessively to himself

Sometimes
he tries to tear away
strips of sunlight from the ashphalt
or attempts to empty
the sandpit with a tea strainer

Mainly
he watches
from between the gaps in his fingers
for keys turning in locks
or a latch left off
the gate

Otherwise
he spends his time
endlessly
looking towards the sky

for that hole in the ozone layer
to run through

JULES LEIGH KOCH

ISAAC THE UNCHOSEN ONE

In a post-modern world who am i
to say she is wrong?
it's all relative isn't it?

He's a kid who will drive you crazy
can't sit still
shouts out whatever drifts into his head

he's five, going on two.
his mother had no parenting skills
& a litany of failed relationships

one guy said *this kid's outa control.*
You gotta choose   him or me.
She chose a new partner.

left the kid with her parents.
He knows he was abandoned.
But morality is relative

and anything goes,
doesn't it?

It is easy not to like him
he could spend an hour
studying a fly or

removing its wings
or making it into a large flat spot.
He will sneeze in his hands
and analyse the snot.

It is easy to like him
like a puppy who knows not
what he does.
lives in the moment

without thought for consequence
tomorrow or
the rest of his life.

rob walker

AT TWELVE

One minute she is galloping
her grown-up body
through long-grassed paddocks
neighing like a horse and laughing
as the dog snaps her heels
or squatting next to the muddy dam
whilst fishing for tadpoles and frog spawn
or digging up worms.

The next minute she is clip-clopping
in high-heeled shoes
straightening her long mane of hair
and thinking about colour
or washing a mud-mask from her face
digging dirt from her fingernails
then polishing and filing them
into adult shape.

SHARON KERNOT

PUBERTY

Glinting eyes, dazzling smiles
cutting wit, subtle wiles,
charming laughs, wilful glances,
sly remarks, provoking stances.

Preening, baiting, what a tease;
trap sprung, next please.

BRIAN FOX

TEENAGE RETREAT

He is like smoke
I cannot grasp
cannot see through –

a thick fog of torment.

I can smell his presence
but he is untouchable
often unfathomable –

a lazy, hazy mystery.

Occasionally he materialises
and we might fight a fire
together

but then he will vanish

burn and smoulder
or spontaneously combust
and once again become a cloud

of uncertainty.

SHARON KERNOT

VOICES

In the days when children
were seen and not heard
my words were mute
my voice, empty
unable to by-pass the invisible
(and arbitrary) line
that accompanied a shotgun glare
or a clip-around-the-ear.

My fingers have learnt
to speak for me.

My own children's self esteem
appears bullet-proof
their words sure-fire.
They open their mouths
and hurl their voices out
into the world.
It seems there is no line
invisible or otherwise.

No one will shoot them down
with ease, least of all me.

SHARON KERNOT

PAPER OF THE TREE
(for Dad)

There is a moon crescent –
Smudged tar over starry sky –
On the other side of the world my father writes
On similar paper, paper of the tree.

Perhaps the motions of our handy scrawl
Could counteract each other's earth twist –
I do not know;

On the other side of the world my father writes
On paper of the tree.

THEODOR W. SCHAPEL

MOTHER'S NEW KITCHEN

She's in the thrall of black and white tiles.
Not the black of night and dirt,
but of shiny polished black dancing shoes.

The white tiles create a divine aura,
a cleanliness of perfection,
the feeling of godless material grace,
that awes her into midnight meditations
on the placement of furniture and cutlery.

The floor's been stripped bare,
like a soul confessing,
as it is repolished and made proud
of its new found wooden honesty.

We the family await for the first dinner,
as children before first confirmation,
where we will worship at this altar of
pagan domesticity.

JULIET PAINE

ARGYLE STEPS

I found him at the bottom of stairs,
framed by an arch.
The caption read: 'Details unknown
but the scene is recognisably the Argyle Steps
in Argyle St the Rocks. Mid 1930s'

But as far as I knew he had never been to Sydney.
For Christ sake he was born in 1932 in Calabria Italy.
But here he stood a grown man wearing an overcoat,
hessian in texture and dumbbell in shape;
riding down to the knees.
Nervous fingers protrude
from this wrinkled bloated coat
stuck like an ice block on two slanted legs
which sit in black leather shoes;
as far as I can see polished without holes,
though the underside of life is always hard to see.

He wasn't wearing a hat,
more it seemed a fedora had grown wings,
a grey plume with Petersham band
had perched itself upon his head,
nesting in time and space
not as permanent as the nearby lamp post
nor solid as the pasted
and stuccoed street upon which he stands.

This is a grey world, pressed between water
which trickles down stone steps into open street
and the twenty five stones
which lay the mouth of a Roman Arch;
pressed between the black and white of family lore;
and the pattern of the rising sun
which like a wallpaper colours the face of this cave:
just another lamp post to the passer by.

Here, where corridor is cut through rock;
he bundles the lip of each step
like loose change into the pocket of an overcoat;
his eyes rest on each step
as if it were a landing between floors:
he stops at the fifteenth landing
where step washes into shadow:
where the past abuts the backward glance:
had only he and I both grasped
the handrail of future and past.

I had spent years searching for that photo of my father,
through bookshop newspapers and old journals,
in an attempt to find the man;
corroborate his fate;
stand as lamp post and street,
face to face so that we might speak.

But a photo is like a lapsed memory;
faults ignored and cracks filled in
and puttied with what we want to see.
I make the best of what is at hand;
as I guess he did before me.

GAETANO AIELLO

ON THE SCRAP HEAP

Every time it fell apart,
we stuck him back together
with sticky tape.
My brother swept up the broken glass,
I took him to the local clinic
& got him bandaged up.
Hid a couple of sleeping tablets
within a milky cup of tea
& watched him pass out on the couch.

Mum had long since left
packed her bags
& fled to her sister's place in Perth,
by the time my brother was 16
& I was old enough to vote.
She reckoned we could fend
for ourselves.
She'd done her bit
tried to mend the old man
like he was a frayed bit of cloth
& failed.
So she threw him out.

Whether it was the sound
of the sea rescue chopper flying overhead
that sent him scrambling
under the coffee table,
or a car backfiring
that punctuated his anxiety
with a sharp exclamation mark.
Sent him swearing at shadows
& making a long day appointment with
his psychiatrist, Jack Daniels.

Sometimes he'd laugh,
look at me in my combat boots,
camouflage pants & Che Guevara ideals,
& tell me I could have been a soldier boy
like him.
I was of the right age
– legal to drink
– legal to drive,
– legal to shoot another man and watch him die.

Eventually it got too much, the pot boiled over
& he didn't come home.
Instead a traffic cop knocked at the door one night,
reported a 1983 rusted red Holden ute overturned
& gift wrapping a local gum tree.

He'd been completely full-stopped.

No longer needing to use his shaky hands
each day to pick his mind & heart up again,
stick them back in his body
& pretend.

JULIET PAINE

TAPHRAYA

My father brought me back orchids from Singapore
wrapped and boxed so carefully that
none of the tender petals were bruised.
Purple and mauve they are, velvet petals,
on strong green stems.

I used to wander down to the market, once,
to buy the smaller sister of these.
I used to wander down to the market
fight the flies and the stench and the heat.

Oppressive, heavy, humid heat
crushing the lungs, but not
these orchids
somehow they were always fresh
in their buckets.

I was different then . . .

My father brought me back orchids from Singapore
perhaps he knows what I remember
and how I anguished for the common rose.

SARAH WAUCHOPE

PISS

often when i piss
i see my own name
written in yellow
or clear ribbons
against the bowl

or sounding out the syllables
in a splash of water

stephen
s
    t
e
     p
h

    e

n

all of my life
everyday
I piss the name
my mother
taught me.

STEVE BROCK

SATURDAY VISIT

In this place of melting moments
seized years
the calendar always shows Thursday.
Soft stew for a spoon fed woman.

Seized years,
the yellowed photographs warp.
Soft stew for a spoon fed woman
on wheels.

The yellowed photographs warp
in her clamped hand
on wheels
below the sunflower sun.

In her clamped hand
fingers unfold questions
below the sunflower sun
in the courtyard smelling of butts.

Fingers unfold questions
I cannot answer.
In the courtyard smelling of butts
she still holds on to faith

I cannot answer.
The calendar always shows Thursday.
She still holds on to faith
In this place of melting moments

LYNETTE ARDEN

UNDER ANDROMEDA

Under Andromeda
beneath a liquid Sunday sky
we wheel you out into the park
Marjory, Mother of Grace
your mind turning
galactic in emptiness
light years from home.

Andromeda hangs low
burnt to the invisible
by the bright light
of day, jocular
with couples, dogs and prams

but its spiral arms cartwheel
godzillions of godzillions of tonnes
carrying perhaps-dinosaurs, maybe-fish, and other
helplessly advanced life-forms
as back on Fullarton Lutheran Rest Home
for the Mentally Ethereal
your wheelchair sticks
in a gutter of stars.

JOHN RICE

EMPTY ROOM

All done, all packed and folded up,
the knick-knacks distributed.

Only her glasses are on the bench.

SALT
of tears
of amniotic fluid

still connected

after all

this

time.

BELINDA BROUGHTON

IT'S MOTHER'S DAY AGAIN

dust her off the shelf
take her out to tea
give her chrysanthemums
and chocolates
and chat ever so politely
yes it's mother's day again

15th SEPTEMBER 2007

the clivea in my front garden
stopped flowering
four years ago
when my lover died
now is once again
in full bloom

G.M. WALKER

GREEN FLOOR

The bliss of anticipation
has me sanding the floor
to protect his imagined white perfect feet.
While I jag my hand on these nails,
these splinters.
I paint the floor green.
And again.
And the next room.
But he doesn't come.
Someone else, squirming,
kicks over the lamp
strews the floor with shards of glass
dangerous as jealousy.
I vacuum them away.
The neighbour's roses send an irrelevant confetti
of parched petals under the door to me.
The earth sends its last fertile centimetre
the moths die dancing for our joy.
If he shows, now,
the meadow I made him
another dusty embarrassment.

A.M. SLADDIN

MY BROTHER'S MAGAZINES

When I was ten
I found my brother's magazines
with the naked women
squeezing their breasts together.

I put them back quickly
but did a little drawing
of a woman in lace
with bare breasts.

Then I tore it up
into very small peices
and ran off
down the back behind the tank

where my hands found
a wet and secret place of me
shocked and delighted
by the shivers.

Then I went to the feed shed
and sat in cool grain
with my bare legs
and my mind turned

to more important matters
like feeding the chooks

BELINDA BROUGHTON

CATULLUS 11

Whether Catullus will go
to far-flung shore of Indres' flow
where Eastern wave with endless roar
pounds earth, and surges back again.

Or whether he will see
the distant tribe of Hyrcani,
soft-living Arabs, countless others,
the endless plains which Nile discolours.

Or whether he will climb
across high Alps in Caesar's wake
the conquered Rhine and furthest Britain
sought through the rough expanse of sea.

Wherever he will go,
    whatever heaven brings,
go back to Rome; say to his girl
these brief and bitter things.

That none she truly loves
for those in her embrace
their juice sucked dry, she drains them all
three hundred in one place.

His love falls far away
like flower by field's edge
left by a plough which slices through
then passing by, is gone.

JACQUELINE CLARKE
Translated from the Latin

CATULLUS 69

Don't cease to wonder why, my Rufus
no girl will spread her legs beneath you
no matter how you try to tempt
with lucid gem or cloth so fine
A certain rumour does you harm
that 'smelly goat' dwells in your arm
and this beast so fierce and rank
no self-respecting tart whould 'shank'!
So kill this pestilence of noses
or cease to ponder flight of floozzies.

JACQUELINE CLARKE
Translated from the Latin

BODY PARTS (4) Knees

Knees bend
and there's the rub.

Apart from being useful for walking
and having dimples in when you are an infant

knees can be humiliating
and hard work:

think of scrubing floors
approaching the boss on hands and knees

bending the knee to the Almighty
and to the more secular Powerful.

Genuflecting.

And then there's arthritis
and water on the knee.

Mind you
I used to like having my knees tickled:

and they are nice curling up in bed with –
or lying like spoons with another pair of knees.

Especially in the winter.

BETTY COLLINS

WASTE

I line the kitty-litter tray
with faces of brides and grooms
smiling from Saturday's news.
Being a recent divorcee,
it says it all really.

JUDE AQUILINA

SUGAR AND SPITE

I know blood's thicker than water, Honey
Don't rub salt into my wounds.
I wasn't quite ripe for the dungheap, Sugar
You threw me out far too soon.

It won't make the pill any sweeter, Baby
If you say your mother was right;
I know I'm no Prince Charming, Darling
But you're not exactly Snow White.

I'm not quite the dish that you ordered, Sweetheart
But next time you won't be so proud
'Cause I'm the real salt of the earth, Honey
And you're just the piss in the clouds.

JULIE WAKEFIELD

'ALL MY CATHODE LOVIN'

"I'm home!"
You walk in the door and for a moment we are nothing but petroleum smiles and blue eyed values – then you take off your shirt and show me the flea-infested monkey fused Siamese-style to your spine. You seem to think this has something to do with me – or worse my mother – just because I happen to be a witch masquerading as a wholesome blonde housewife named Samantha (leading to all manner of zany situations and good clean family entertainment).

You say you're sick of all this. You wish I'd just stop being a witch masquerading as a wholesome blonde housewife named Samantha (leading to all manner of zany situations and good clean family entertainment). As you speak the lighting softens, I find myself telling you, *No, don't be ridiculous, I can't be anything other than what I am.*

Which is rather ironic because I'm suddenly taller and dark-haired and male . . . and I am Victor Newman from '*The Young And The Restless*'; you are plastered with make-up, blonde wig back to front, you are Nikki or Ashley or it doesn't really matter, you are sobbing, saying you can't go on. I remain firm, unbending, intolerant, cold, telling you to pull yourself together – this is humiliating.

You respond with a roundhouse and flying kickflip, which I dodge because I am Catwoman and you are Batman – obviously. Our lounge room walls are flashing with pop art explosions POW! BAM! BIFF! ZAM!

Then, in the middle of it all this bald guy rocks up, and starts laying into us both. We've got no choice but to join forces against him, which we do and he pummels us both whilst the studio audience chants STEVE STEVE STEVE!!!!

Because we are contestants on '*The Jerry Springer Show*' and today's topic is, '*Yes, I love you, but not as much as I love midget porn*'. The worst part is neither of us have ever watched midget porn, which makes Jerry very unhappy. He says we've ruined his entire reputation. I feel so sorry and ashamed, all I can do is bury my head in my knees and cry . . .

When I finally look up I realize I am clinically obese. Panicking, I glance at you, gain sadistic relief to see you've suffered the same. Now we're on '*Dr Phil*' and he's doing his Tough Love tactics, telling us this is all our own faults: we need to wake up and take responsibility.

So we pool together all our strength to try to be Kylie Minogue and Jason Donovan playing Scott and Charlene in the original '*Neighbours*', but the best we can do is be Scott and Charlene on a '*Neighbours*' reunion special. You're Jason Donovan the washed-up addict and I'm not even Kylie Minogue.

You come right out and say, *That was pathetic*, and I say, *No it wasn't*, not because I don't think it was pathetic, but because I like to disagree with everything you say, because you're David Stratton and I'm Margaret Pomeranz and we both know, deep down, we should never have left SBS.

It's too late now. Larry Emdur is standing in our kitchen, we're guessing at the value of Fridge, Microwave, Toaster . . .but the price is wrong, we both lose, and a metrosexual law student from Sydney takes home the lot.

We make for the liquor cabinet, but Johnny Young has been their first and is teetering atop the lounge suite preparing to sing . . .

AMELIA WALKER

UNTOUCHED

And he was untouched by all this
He had fucked the night away
and was down the beach,
joking spermatozoically in the sand.

And she was untouched by all this
She had fucked the night away
and was down the beach
drenching the air with her virginity

KAHIL JUREDINI

UN JUST: LIKE A GIRL

I took the incest
like a girl.
I took the insults
like a girl.
I took the rape
like a girl.
I took to self-abnegation
like a girl.
I took to drugs
like a girl.
I took dinner orders
like a girl.
I took to the drink
like a girl.
I took out the washing
like a girl.
I took him for a ride
under & on & near the table
like a girl.
I took it all.
Just.
Like a woman.

A.M. SLADDIN

IN THE OXFORD ETYMOLOGICAL DICTIONARY

I go back to Greek
loving the language
that gives me writing

'Graphos', writing –
writing with light
takes me into
photography

And from the
eye to the ear
comes the sound
of the phonograph.

And writing across
unmeasured distance
unseen, immediate
telegraphy.

And Greeks have
a word too for
writing imprinted
forever indelible

unable to be erased
foul, loathsome,
written in blood
pain and tears

graphic in horror
written in flesh
torn to please
brutes who buy

from profiteers
making money out
of people – just things
for pornography.

ERICA JOLLY

DOING IT IN BED

An English Professor
boasted to me once
that at any one time
between him and his wife
they had around three hundred books
in the bedroom.
Upon arriving home
I made a quick inventory of texts:
poems by Blaise Cendrars
the bible in Spaish translation
Mario Benedetti's *Collected Poems*
a first edition of *Notes of a Dirty Old Man*
Isabel Allende's *Eva Luna*
some picture books
including a porno under the bed
from the time my best man
was assistant editor of *Hustler* magazine
and perhaps a half a dozen other titles
I couldn't be bothered recounting here.
Mostly we spent the time there
sleeping or fucking.

STEVE BROCK

ON A 'GOOD NIGHT'. (DARLING)

Each night

now

darling

we bed our favourite loves.

Piss,

Pot,

and masturbation's glove.

A.M. SLADDIN

PENTECOSTAL

Without his God
his Pentecostal God
he would have picked them up
from the strip under the flightpath
& driven them out to the outdoor places
he knew like the back of his hands
the forest, the blackberries
the blue, evergreen river
& before driving them back
with his money filling their next high
under the jetstream, he
would have fucked them
three times a day
sometimes

but
with his God
his Pentecostal God
he was affronted by them
so outraged by them strung out along the strip
he often complained to his neighbours
before & after he fucked them &
pulled twine or fishing line
or their clothing
tight
around their necks
or
both at once.

GRAHAM ROWLANDS
Joint Website Poem of the Month: August

SONG OF SEPARATION

You are
my Guantanamo Bay
baby

I can only reach you
by mail

I can only touch you
with words

No gifts
are allowed

No hugs
are possible

I ask permission
to see you
and am denied

You are
my Guantanamo Bay
baby

You've been
detained
And she's never gonna let you
come home.

JUDY DALLY

SEARCH FOR MR RIGHT

Apparently it's official,
the search for Mr Right
has been abandoned.

After due consideration –
one Vodka Cranberry Tonic,
two Manhattans –

there's nothing left to do
but smoke your last cigarette
outside;

line up the Tequila shots
with lemon wedges
and salt;

and after two hours
of rigorous hip-like-a-ho
Beyonce butt – dancing

to loud Techno repe-ti-tive beat;
avoiding all football players
and other women dis-respectors;

accept a ride home
with a halfway decent
Mr Right Now.

M.L. EMMETT

I AM A REFLECTION IN A SHOP WINDOW

I am a reflection in a shop window
I live in a house of cards.
I eat paper bread;
I drink coloured wine.

By day I shred words and mince phrases;
at night I screw up my thoughts
into tight tissue balls
and pack them neatly
in grey cardboard boxes
on white plastic shelves.

Then I curl up in my feather bed
and lie in wait for oblivion.

But closing my lids does not shut out
the writhing world within.

I dread the night's blackness.
Its monsters are far more substantial
than pale daylight's shadows.
I hear Night's creatures
hissing in my ears:
one night I will be sucked away
flesh, bones and marrow
into reality.

The morning sun will find
the shadow of a face upon my pillow.

JULIE WAKEFIELD

UNTITLED

I could write
about lost love

or constant depression

I could write about punching
angry holes in the door

or about screaming abuse
at arseholes who had it comin'

But my psych
has doped up to the eyeballs
on mood stabilisers

and that shit is real gooood.

DANIEL WILSON

LONELINESS

the sharp
stab-wound
of loneliness
catches breath
stills voice
as thumb-press
on larynx

cells recoil
draw in
blood vessels
constrict
to slow
the seeping
life-flow

wrap another
plaster bandage
to harden
and hide
mask-like
behind
painted eyes
and smile.

VERONICA SHANKS
Website Poem of the Month: March

art form

sit by the window. type with one hand till the prozac takes
hold. drop out to your alter ego 'strap-on girl'. take on the
world with your sinister sister. paint pictures in porn.
establish galleries of eyeball scraping masterpieces. break
through the barriers of depravity and find fame in the
strangest of places.

angels speak in fingers and tongues like deaf people. you
are secretly suspicious of the handicapped. refuse to learn
their language. still their sounds loop through your mind like
a skip rope rhyme. your shadow slumps in the corner,
exhausted, the little egos that you nurture in the window box
are struggling in the winter sun, your guts feels like a traffic
jam of fire engines. oh the humanity.

plagued by impossibilities, you obsess with pretensions at
company. leave the door creaking. read dead lovers' love
letters. use comfort puppets around the lounge room and
as occasional dance partners. put pillows under the doona,
roll over and pretend that someone's there.

loneliness, like pornography, is an art form.

KERRYN TREDREA

TRUMAN CAPOTE'S QUIRKS

I have to add up numbers, all numbers:
there are some people I never telephone
because their number adds up to unlucky;
ditto, there are hotel rooms I say no to &
no to three cigarette butts in an ashtray.
I won't travel on a plane with two nuns.
They're endless, the things I can't & won't.
I won't begin or end anything on a Friday.
I will not countenance yellow roses — sad
because they're my favourite flowers.

GRAHAM ROWLANDS

AN AESTHETIC MAN

The one-inch rocker with corkscrew grooming
sat cross-legged in strange orchestras crooning:
     electric warrior with larynx of silk,
     with cheeks a-glitter those evenings of damask,
Dandy of the Other World, Warlock of Love, Lord of the Ringlets,
born to boogy through mists of Albany –
     that twentieth century boy was born
     to be my aesthetic unicorn.

Did any of his being not exude
a facet of art or display pulchritude?
     Cascading corkscrew coiffure,
     elegant sartorial allure,
a pretty voice, sweet and light, blithe as a lark,
each sentence fading into whisper at halfway mark,
lyrics barely translated from the language of Fairyland,
melodies as mellifluently penned as by any Mendelssohn's hand,
     mystic mythologist with no flesh for food
     metal minstrel but petal guru.

To live in London in an early seventy
was to know the meaning of T-Rextasy.
     Mark my words:
never again shall we have the chance
To Get it On with such bedazzling Cosmic Dance.

He died as a Childe – on the verge of turning thirty years old.
No birthday honour required for a natural knight of gold!
I don't mean to be bold but I still do hold
     a candle burning Hot Love
for one of the beautiful Children of the Revolution
     my main Telegram Man . . .
     Mister Marc Bolan.

When his voice like a spaceball, richocets up my spine,
I feel his soul come closer and closer to mine,
like a Jeepster I jolt to those sounds from a realm divine,
    like a white swan I see him glide
    and I long to cling to his neck forever to ride
but then, alas and alack, a feeling of loss takes hold,
    and when I'm sad, I slide!

KALICHARAN NIGEL DEY
*Read on the 30th anniversary of the death of Marc Bolan,
lead singer of T. Rex.*

automatonophobia
(fear of ventriloquists'dummies)

they are not to be trusted.
their smiles   fixed.
little quadriplegic arms and legs

flop uselessly or folded like x
over non-ex
istent genitals.

their wooden hearts never feel
a beat,
yet their timing is perfect.

who's a naughty boy?

And you don't want to know
where that man
has his hand . . .

the only words that leave their mouths
those thrown there
by someone else.

after work they retire to lonely hotel rooms,
lie listessly on a bed,
stare vacantly at a ceiling.

or drown the sorrows
of their empty lives
in a gottle of gear.

rob walker
Website poem

PICASSO'S CAT

Picasso's Cat
certainly offered
no angles to the wind
as he stretched
yawned his mouth
the colour of sangria
counted his mistresses
and then

decided to go bird-hunting
instead.

The Demoiselles D'Avignon
could wait.

BEETHOVEN'S CAT

Beethoven's cat
was stone deaf
and liked to sleep
inside the piano

(he covered at least
four octaves)

his aging owner
never
noticed.

AVALANCHE IVAN REHOREK

RAW SIENNA
(For Peg)

I see how years of painting seep
and oil your lifelines with cerise.
Each palm branded and each crease
finely etched, precise and deep.

Your painted mountains are aubergines
hinting at a darker pleasure
and with earthy laughter raw sienna
mixes a salad of bitter greens.

I envy you your singing colours
Sinatra red and Presley purple,
Guy Mitchell blue, all come full circle
from teenage years and long hot summers.

But exuberance is brilliant farce,
a bunch of full and spilling grapes,
the crystal bowl distorting shapes,
sunlight pinging the deep cut glass.

For years I saw but missed the clues,
the tears beneath the bold impasto,
your palette-knife layering shadow
along the edge of rainbow hues.

MARY BRADLEY

THE YUENDUMU DOORS

Exhibited at Tandanya

They're postcards now
and book marks for sale
in the bookshop of the
South Australian Museum

But once they were doors,
doors of class rooms set
on this Aboriginal land
to teach the English tongue.

Not all conquerors
felt it was their right
and duty to stamp out
signs of ancient ways.

While these doors gave
entry to an alien world
this new art teacher
saw them as canvasses.

Walpiri men could paint
their stories on these doors:
their children could take
their heritage into that room.

They'd find in symbols
reminders of their Dreaming
without a single hard-edge
ruled geometrical line.

All curious twists, circles
for waterholes, curves
for women, marks for
kangaroo or falcon tracks,

Language old as stories
told in sand, in boulders,
shooting star, desert oak
and in the Milky Way.

Alive with colours –
ochred red, yellow,
charcoal black and white
painted in lasting oils.

Tales of honey ant
and mulga worm dreaming
mapping soakages and –
only with permission –

tales of women's Dreaming
and of the old man, Possum
sitting alone, near the swamp
at the Place of Dawn.

ERICA JOLLY

PORTRAIT OF THE ARTIST AS A YOUNG LANDSCAPE

(from a painting of the same name by Pamela Lofts)

I

My *kardiya* eyes are drawn
to a dark smudge of scrub
on the straight line of horizon.
I search the bleak landscape;
beyond the weathered smoothness
of two boulders; across the lifeless
expanse of a dull grey, salt pan,
my eyes traversing distorted distance
but the painting appears devoid of life.

II

Then you miss everything, says the artist –
the woman lying on the shore of the dry salt pan
her breasts covered with grey ash.
The shadowed indentation of her navel,
the gentle rise of her soft belly,
the dense thicket of her pubic mound.
This landscape gave me birth
and from between the boulders of her
upraised knees I first saw
the shimmering mirage of distance.

MARY BRADLEY

kardiya = white

ULURU HAIKU

Beat of creation
ridge of consciousness
time and place waiting.

                                    Resonance of rock
                                    striations of story
                                    bare-faced with time.

Skin of consciousness
unwrinkles another dream
opens with time.

                                    Line of tumbled rock
                                    canyon of an ancient dream
                                    spinal column.

Encircling arms
gather us into the earth
our destination.

                                    Drought drives despair
                                    hope pitter patters my roof
                                    evaporates.

MAEVE ARCHIBALD

DROUGHT

Dipped in thioadldehyde
appendages amputated
the retreat from life
washed into the knotted trunks
of twelve trees which stand as piers;
pylons driven into the deep
bolt the bough of an empty hay shed
to the blue sky.
The cladding of permanence
tractor fertilizer harvester
stalks of wheat tethered
like beached hulks
to a bone dry dock.

GAETANO AIELLO

HI-JACKED

homestead veranda salutes
the legacy of farmers
who battled drought and absent rain
and lost

nature their silent partner
climate hi-jacked by el Ninio
equal shares in hardship

paddocks stock empty
working dogs idle
lying in kennels

Raven wings flap
black arm bands worn
at the funeral
of barren stock and crops.

COLLEEN SWEENEY

THE DRY WELL

The old man runs his gnarled hands
through sparse white hair.
He turns on the tap, a trickle,
then a vacant gurgle.
Well's run dry he sighs.
He has held out as long as he could.
A gust of wind sends tumbleweed
and memories adrift.

Faded blue eyes look into the distance:
a distant past, no longer his.
He stands and surveys the garden
spreading out from his feet.
The meandering path draws his eyes
through an abundance of leafy greens
festooned with colour
flowers of all shapes and sizes
yellow, pink, mauve and lilac.
His wife's favourite colurs.
Her blooms adorned the oak table
in the chipped green vase.
He can hear the snip of her garden shears
the lifting lilt of her voice in song.
For a while he drifts in their past . . .

Then the lonely caw of a crow brings him back
from the garden in his mind
Gone, all gone now he sighs again
turns his back
and shuffles inside.

INEKE BOS

NIGHT SHADE

Past the creek, in wild oats,
Headstones jut at different angles,
All their inscriptions worn away.

There's still warmth in the white road,
But the sky where a summer moon hangs
Is cold as trough-water at break of day.

When the wind shifts, dry grass
Could be distant sea, or a thousand ghosts
Whispering through their hollow bones,

But the only ripples the creek has passed
Are shadows cast by rotten posts
And the tread-pattern a long drought has sown,

And the only ghost to whisper is me,
An empty head in empty space
Waiting for its resurrection to come,

Trying to remember a shiny sea,
Laughter, goose-bumps, a loving face,
Dreams glimpsed in flickers of sun.

GEOFF KEMP

DEFIANCE
(a Kyrielle for Erica)

That gum-tree leaning on the fence
was clearly worrying the nice neighbour
he'd often look over with a calculating eye
(for a tree will grow where it can)

That spoke of axes and chainsaws
so the final day came, well, finally –
the men sweltered and sliced the trunk into wafers
for a tree will grow where it wants

laid them out in the garden like wooden pavers –
then made sure the stump was good and dead
with poison and fire as a final solution;
for a tree will grow where it must

but even as the charred surfaces turned grey
the slightest spray of green came on
blushing then powering from buds to leaves
for a tree can grow where it wants

finally a glorious forest blazed out, defiant
for a tree must grow where it must
no amount of petrol and weed killer can overcome now –

for a tree will grow where it will.

AVALANCHE IVAN REHOREK
Website Poem of the Month: December

LICHEN IN THE STATION

circles of crusty lichen
spatter the platform
flat and dull, these rusty coins
cling fast to life on asphalt

circles of pale grey lichen
withstand a thousand steps a day
kicked by sneakers
stuck by stilettos
quietly smothered by thick tan loafers

circles of shrivelled lichen
surrounded by tickets and spent chewing gum
hiding their life
they face the sun
draw air and rain
and grow on, in defiance

J.L. BAKER

THE GAGGLE

On the distant hillside they are
a string of white seed pearls slinking
down to the still mirror of pond.

After a splash-bath they groom
themselves on the bank, twisting their
pipe-cleaner necks into impossible angles.

Every feather is teased as their teeth
comb and pluck out tufts of white fluff
until the grass has a light snow-fall.

When all quills are pure, they plop down
on ample behinds, tuck their heads
neatly beneath their wings and fall asleep.

They are a fleet of freshly painted boats
moored to a patch of mid-morning sun.
One of them always keeps an eye on the world.

At a gust of wind, or a passing car, it honks
and it's up periscope, all in quick succession
as if a fox rippled through their dreams.

JUDE AQUILINA
Website Poem of the Month: May

GREY PLUNDER

In my hand
loose feather down

soft remains

soft like fleece
soft like velvet, soft
like silk still floating
still fleeing
silent stalking

In my hand
softness gathered
In my hand
warmth grows

In my hand
Regret

GENNY DREW

LIZARD

in the glare
of the hot sun
it catches my eye

as it basks
on the terra cotta wall
soaking up summer

its body
strangely translucent
in the light

lies frozen
hooded eyes
unblinking

as i edge closer
its chest palpitates
with fear

its tail untwists
as it darts
for safety

leaving only a
rustle
in the undergrowth

JILL GOWER
Maureen Vale Competition: Commendation

BAT IN A PANTRY

You're home at last from the night shift,
hanging from the handle of the coffee grinder
by your micro grapple-hook feet.

If only those humans wouldn't flit in and out,
clicking that annoying little sun,
and must they make so much noise?

Your ears minutely swivel, even in your sleep,
rich fur is bunched about your neck –
'bald mouse' how dare they name you so!

You are a beautiful baby buggy,
leather hood folded down
struts fine-boned for the sky.

When darkness eases in.
you will leave this cardamon-heavy air
and fly against the lacework of the stars

into the webbed dreams
of pantry keepers,
tossing, flightless, on their beds.

MIKE LADD

RAIN

All day clouds were spilling
over the Barossa hills –
puce, grey, then grey to black, climbing
the sky towards dusk – every
action like a strained foreboding;
cicada screaming at a broad hooked moon;

but it was well past midnight
when the rain struck:
a fierce, defiant drumming on the roofs,
that woke us, laid us back
through countless minutes,
as though beneath hard beating hooves;

gasping, we struggled to the window,
glimpsed only blackness, gaped
unbelief that such determined drenchings
could be so wholly curtained by the darkness,
lie just as hidden in the morning
the brown land drained and dry
as though not one drop had fallen –

that drumming just a trick of all our fears,
detritus of some dark conclusion;
all day, our eyes were fixed on the horizon;
puce, grey, then grey to black –
as something nameless climbed the years.

RON PHILLIPS

RIVER TREES

we follow the road
as it winds beside the Murray
silvered branches mirrored on its surface

dying eucalypts half-submerged
flounder in the river's flood
only their limbs above the water

not waving but drowning

JILL GOWER

HAIKU

Fragile liaison . . .
balanced on trembling green leaf
a water droplet.

GENNY DREW

Circles on water –
Spring with fallen rain elates
Tadpoles into Frogs

PAUL SUTTON

AFTER RAIN

Leaves of plants
stretch a little higher
brighter darker
the wide straps of the clivia
arch glistening
athletes poised for the race
the last drops sit
on the leaves
like a prayer

ROS SCHULZ

REASONING

as I lift the blind
to look out the window
to let in light

left-over raindrops
that won't fall to the ground
are jewelled in the diosma
under the bottle-brush tree

which reminds me

it's the queen's birthday
giving us this chance
to watch sunlight from the bed

in midwinter

on a quiet monday

in the morning

DAVID MORTIMER

SAND

I built a house of sand
grain by careful grain
a memorial to some
wordless thought
some thoughtless holding.
It will be demolished
fast or slow, by wind and water
and by activities
human and inhuman.

I understand now, a little
of what monks teach.

We are all here to form our patterns
and be swept away
transformed
like sea on sand.

Our bodies and our minds
slow mandalas
the thought, the map
the substance
the transfiguremernt.

If your body is
the shadow of your thought,
where is the light?

JO DEY

LOOKING AT BOATS

Fishing boat at sea,
fly speck on glass

Silver wakes like snails,
boats surge hungrily out to sea
lured by the songs of Nereids.

Water hits the barnacled keel,
a blue-green silence
dense as fear amongst whipping sea grass.

Sun reflects like a thousand stars
on the water. Fishermen
drop anchor, rock sleepily,
ignore its startling beauty.

A boat breaks the blue thread
of the long, thin horizon
stretching taut, like string.

For twenty years a dream;
he hooks the giant flathead,
now, eye to eye,
lets it go,
pulls anchor.

Cling to the small boat's lurching sides,
succumb to the sea's exquisite torture.

TESS DRIVER

KAYAKING ~ FOR PATRICIA IRVINE

The day is green,
the light at the edge of clouds
sobering the river.
Mangrove blossom
scents the air with a bouquet
like the bottom of a fruit crate –
something tropical, yet wood-slat.

Sleek and lustrous and slimy grey,
a mother dolphin and her calf
farm the shallows,
backs arching down and again down,
driving glimmers of silver
from Port River weed.

Swan Alley, Shooting Creek,
The Cutting: our kayaks
slap the chop or glide into shush
to hear the invisible wren,
the loping croaks of white-faced heron.

Emerging from reflected acres of leaf
to where the powerlines hum,
we approach industrial heaven:
sculptural wrecks, gantries, derricks,
the hooded brontosaurial rust –
Jonahs inside the ribs of echoing whales.

Around the point, the wind turns
and we work to a more-distant shore,
pushing in rhythm, like gangers or lovers.
A pair of sharp-tailed sandpipers
startle from the bank –
Autumn is coming
and all the miles to Siberia.

MIKE LADD

THE SEA, THE SEA

This morning I find the sea
meditating again,
rolling its shameless mantras onto the shore,
and scattering messages of peace
into unwary ears.

JO DEY

FIND A JAPANESE HAIKU AT MIDDLETON BEACH

Wind and waves.
Seagulls at Middleton Beach.
Feet are pencils writing in the wet sand.

After a few waves
the afternoon comes.
Shore and solitude.
I am reading with pleasure
The moonlight is my only lamp at sea.

JUAN GARRIDO-SALGADO

ESPLANADE

Edge of the sea

is

peaceful

like

a

nesting

animal

digging

earth.

ALGAE CALLIGRAPHY

There are clouds
over the sea.
And drifts of seaweed.
Writing in the clouds
like finger prints
in foggy windows.
And in the drifts
of seaweed
calligraphy.

JAYNE LINKE

twilight

silhouettes become darker

                                           gradually

against

                                           a pale pink and blue sky

mysteries deepen

amongst subtleties

                    of texture

                            and wistfulness

                              SALLY ANN HUNTER

EVENING UNFOLDS

Delicate flowers

bloom
in the
sky.

A bold
sunset-sideshow.

JAYNE LINKE

DELUGE

Prolonged rumblings from the clouds
work loose the tangles in my brain
of yesterday's choices
and tomorrow's consequences.

Massaging rain on the tin roof
unknots my shoulders and back
and dissolves hard lumps
in my calves and thighs
caused by sleeping on buses
and waiting in bus stations.

Adiabatics nullify the tropical latitudes
bringing coldness in the night;
I leave open the window to let you in
pushing through the curtains on the breeze.
The rustle of draperies is the sound of you
tossing lightly in bed beside me.

I snuggle into the early morning storm
feeling the warmth of you
and willing suspension of time;
like a persistent alarm
the last trickle rattling in the downpipe
wakes me.

Uneven dripping on the broad-leafed canopy
draws me to the louvered window
where the first truck changing-down on the hill
hauls me into the day.

ROGER HIGGINS

For futher information about
Friendly St publications and activities please visit
www.friendlystreetpoets.org.au
or write to
email: poetry@friendlystreetpoets.org.au
postal: PO Box 43, Rundle Mall, Adelaide SA 5000